ROAD TRIP
TRIVIA

Published by Willow Creek Press, Inc.
P.O. Box 147, Minocqua, Wisconsin 54548

Printed in the United States

ROAD TRIP
TRIVIA

OFFBEAT FACTS FOR THE OFFBEATEN PATH

✦ WILLOW CREEK PRESS®

SUNTAN LOTION
WAS INVENTED
IN FLORIDA.

"TAKE ME HOME, COUNTRY ROADS"
IS NOT ONLY A GREAT ROAD TRIP SONG,
IT'S THE OFFICIAL STATE SONG OF
WEST VIRGINIA.

OREGON HAS OVER 80 GHOST TOWNS
ON THE NATIONAL REGISTER.

CALIFORNIA'S REDWOOD
NATIONAL PARK HAS THE
TALLEST TREES ON THE PLANET.

THE CITY OF NEW ORLEANS, LOUISIANA, IS BELOW SEA LEVEL, REQUIRING CEMETERIES TO CONSTRUCT ABOVE-GROUND TOMBS.

ALASKA IS THE ONLY STATE WITHOUT AN INTERSTATE HIGHWAY. HAWAII HAS THREE (H-1, H-2 AND H-3).

KRISPY KREME DOUGHNUTS WERE FIRST DEVELOPED, BAKED, AND SOLD FROM A SMALL STORE NEAR WINSTON-SALEM, NORTH CAROLINA.

UTAH'S GREAT SALT LAKE IS FOUR TIMES SALTIER THAN ANY OF THE OCEANS.

CARLSBAD CAVERNS
NATIONAL PARK IN NEW
MEXICO IS A DRAW UNTO
ITSELF, BUT THE BONUS
COMES AT SUNSET WHEN UP
TO A HALF-MILLION BATS FLY
OUT OF THE CAVES TO FEED.

ALABAMA'S STATE QUARTER INCLUDES BRAILLE COMMEMORATING NATIVE-BORN HELEN KELLER. HER BIRTHPLACE IS THE TOWN OF TUSCUMBIA WHICH EVERY SUMMER HOSTS PRODUCTIONS OF "THE MIRACLE WORKER."

IDAHO'S CAPITOL BUILDING IS THE ONLY STRUCTURE HEATED BY THERMAL ENERGY FROM UNDERGROUND HOT SPRINGS.

RISING 14,258 FEET, LEADVILLE, COLORADO, IS THE HIGHEST CITY IN THE COUNTRY.

WASHINGTON STATE HAS MULTIPLE VOLCANOES, INCLUDING MT. ST. HELENS, WHICH ERUPTED IN 1980-THE DEADLIEST SUCH EVENT IN U.S. HISTORY.

COTTON CANDY WAS INVENTED IN NASHVILLE, TENNESSEE IN 1904 BY A DENTIST AND A CANDY MAKER.

KANSAS PAYS TRIBUTE TO THE MOVIE CLASSIC, "THE WIZARD OF OZ," WITH A REPLICA OF DOROTHY'S KANSAS HOME AND RECREATIONS OF MOVIE SITES AT THE SEWARD COUNTY CORONADO MUSEUM.

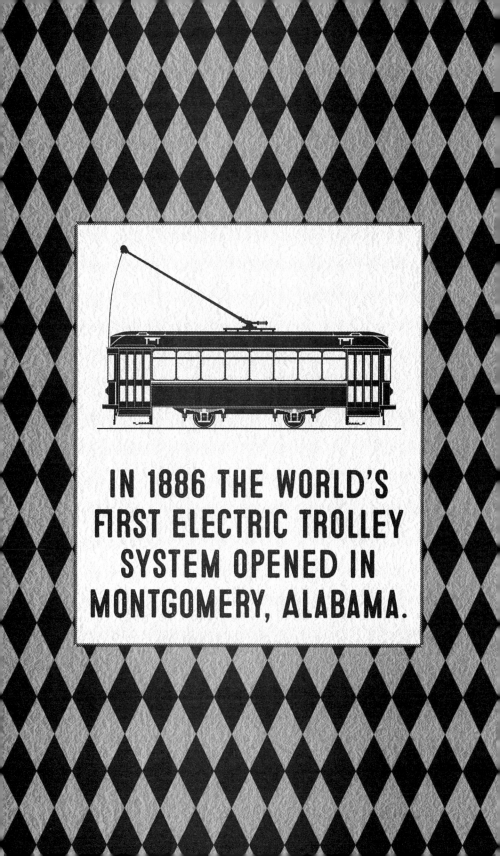

IN 1886 THE WORLD'S FIRST ELECTRIC TROLLEY SYSTEM OPENED IN MONTGOMERY, ALABAMA.

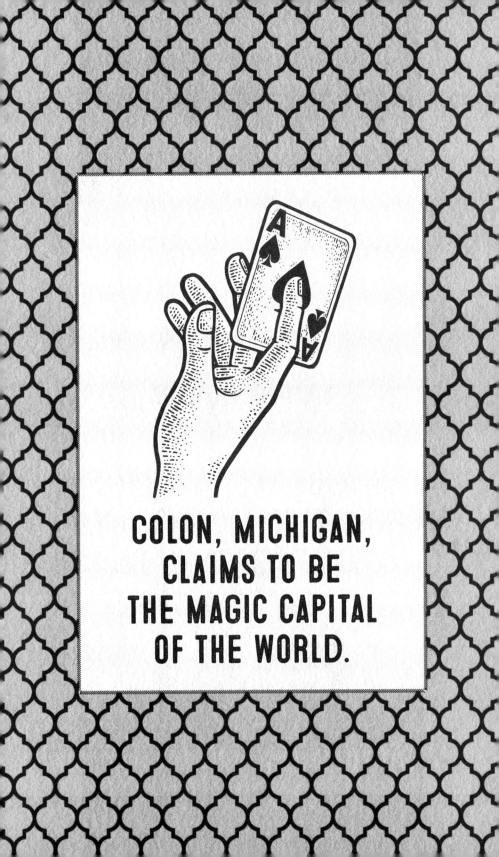

COLON, MICHIGAN,
CLAIMS TO BE
THE MAGIC CAPITAL
OF THE WORLD.

TEXAS' 268,000 SQUARE MILES MAKE IT
LARGER THAN ANY EUROPEAN COUNTRY.

CALIFORNIA HAS A POPULATION
OF MORE THAN 39 MILLION PEOPLE.

NEW MEXICO IS THE ONLY STATE
WITH AN OFFICIAL QUESTION. ASKING
"RED OR GREEN?" REFERS TO WHICH COLOR
OF CHILES A DINER WISHES TO BE SERVED.

ALASKA HAS MORE COASTLINE (34,000 MILES) THAN THE REST OF THE U.S. COMBINED.

THE LOST RIVER CAVE BENEATH BOWLING GREEN, KENTUCKY, FEATURES A SEVEN-MILE CAVE SYSTEM AND FEATURES BOAT AND KAYAK TOURS.

THE FIRST PERSON CHARGED WITH SPEEDING WAS GOING EIGHT MPH.

COCA-COLA WAS
INVENTED IN
ATLANTA, GEORGIA,
IN 1886.

ILLINOIS IS THE LARGEST
PRODUCER OF PUMPKINS
IN THE NATION.

OPENED IN 1887, THE FOXBURY COUNTRY CLUB IN CLARION COUNTY, PENNSYLVANIA, IS THE OLDEST GOLF COURSE IN THE COUNTRY.

THE PRO FOOTBALL HALL OF FAME IS LOCATED IN CANTON, OHIO.

SOUTH CAROLINA STATES, "IT IS UNLAWFUL FOR A MINOR UNDER THE AGE OF 18 TO PLAY A PINBALL MACHINE."

GREEN BAY, WISCONSIN, IS NOT ONLY THE
HOME OF THE PACKERS FOOTBALL TEAM,
IT'S ALSO KNOWN AS THE
"TOILET PAPER CAPITAL OF THE WORLD."

WILMINGTON, DELAWARE, IS HOME TO OLD
SWEDES CHURCH BUILT 1698-1699.

HERSHEY, PENNSYLVANIA, IS THE
CHOCOLATE CAPITAL OF THE U.S. AND
BOASTS NOT ONLY THE FACTORY BUT AN
AMUSEMENT PARK AND CHOCOLATE MUSEUM.

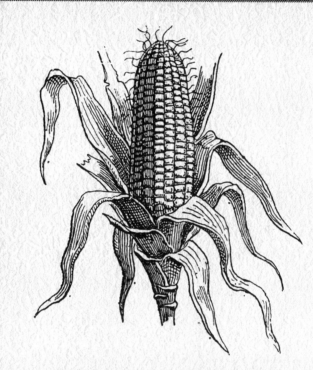

THE CULT CLASSIC
"CHILDREN OF THE CORN"
WAS FILMED
THROUGHOUT IOWA.

SOUTH CAROLINA
PRODUCES THREE
TIMES MORE PEACHES
THAN GEORGIA.

FLORIDA HAS THE LONGEST COASTLINE (1,350 MILES) IN THE CONTIGUOUS U.S. CALIFORNIA IS SECOND.

INTERSTATE HIGHWAYS FREQUENTLY PASS THROUGH MULTIPLE STATES AND KEEP THE SAME IDENTIFYING NUMBER FROM BEGINNING TO END.

THE MISSISSIPPI RIVER IS ONE OF THE NATION'S MOST IMPORTANT MIGRATION ROUTES FOR BIRDS AS WELL AS FISH.

HOT SPRINGS NATIONAL PARK IN HOT SPRINGS, ARKANSAS, HAS HOSTED AN ARRAY OF CELEBRITY VISITORS OVER THE YEARS INCLUDING BABE RUTH, FDR, AND HOMETOWN BOY BILL CLINTON.

ALASKA COVERS A TOTAL AREA OF 663,268 SQUARE MILES MAKING IT THE LARGEST STATE IN LANDMASS.

THE U.S. HIGHWAY INTERSTATE SYSTEM INCLUDES 82 TUNNELS.

IT IS ILLEGAL TO BOX
WITH A KANGAROO IN
MYRTLE CREEK, OREGON.

THE STATUE OF LIBERTY
STANDS 305 FEET FROM
HEAD TO FOOT AND
WEARS A SIZE 879 SHOE.

DR. CHARLES BROWN FLEET OF LYNCHBURG, VIRGINIA, INVENTED CHAPSTICK IN THE 1880S.

THE NEW ORLEANS SAINT CHARLES STREETCAR LINE AND THE SAN FRANCISCO CABLE CARS ARE OUR ONLY MOBILE NATIONAL MONUMENTS.

CHARLOTTE, NORTH CAROLINA, IS HOME TO THE NASCAR HALL OF FAME AND IS OPEN TO THE PUBLIC.

JUST SOUTH OF PHILO, OHIO, SITS THE
EARTH-FRIENDLY ABODE DUBBED THE
"HOUSE OF TRASH." IT'S MADE
ENTIRELY OF RECYCLED MATERIALS.

FLORIDA IS THE FLATTEST
STATE IN THE NATION.

COVERING 28 MILLION ACRES,
ADIRONDACK PARK IS THE LARGEST
NATIONAL PARK IN THE CONTIGUOUS U.S.

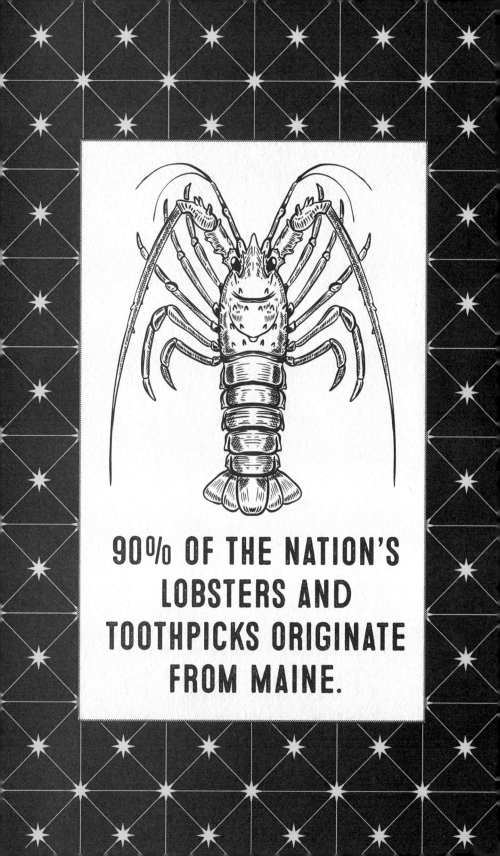

90% OF THE NATION'S LOBSTERS AND TOOTHPICKS ORIGINATE FROM MAINE.

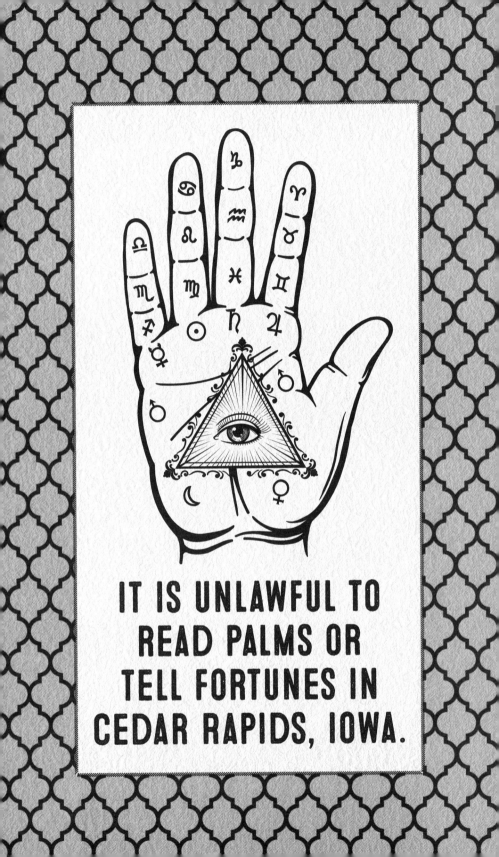

IT IS UNLAWFUL TO
READ PALMS OR
TELL FORTUNES IN
CEDAR RAPIDS, IOWA.

CHILI IS THE OFFICIAL STATE DISH OF TEXAS.

VIRGINIA HAS THE MOST CONFEDERATE MEMORIALS IN THE U.S.

A FEW MILES OUT OF CHESTNUT HILL, TENNESSEE, SITS THE BUSH'S BAKED BEAN MUSEUM WHICH DRAWS 1,000 SUMMER VISITORS DAILY.

IN 1901 CONNECTICUT WAS THE FIRST STATE
TO POST AUTOMOBILE SPEED LIMITS.
THE LIMITS WERE SET AT 12 MPH IN
CITIES AND 15 MPH ON COUNTRY ROADS.

THE FIRST AND OLDEST THRU-HIKING TRAIL IS
VERMONT'S LONG TRAIL. COMPLETED IN 1930,
IT TRAVERSES 272 MILES.

TINY AND REMOTE SUPAI VILLAGE SITS
AT THE BASE OF THE GRAND CANYON.
IT'S THE ONLY PLACE IN THE NATION
WHERE MAIL IS DELIVERED VIA PACK MULE.

LOUISIANA HAS MORE ALLIGATORS THAN ANY OTHER STATE.

IN CONNECTICUT IT IS
ILLEGAL TO BLOW A
WHISTLE OUTDOORS.

INTERSTATE 97 IS THE SHORTEST INTERSTATE HIGHWAY RUNNING JUST 17.6 MILES FROM ANNAPOLIS TO BALTIMORE.

FORT BRAGG, WEST OF FAYETTEVILLE, NORTH CAROLINA, IS THE LARGEST MILITARY BASE IN THE WORLD.

NEW ORLEANS HAS A GROUP OF "SELF-IDENTIFYING VAMPIRES" WHO RITUALISTICALLY DRINK HUMAN BLOOD FROM WILLING DONORS.

RUSSELL CAVE IN BRIDGEPORT, ALABAMA,
BECAME A NATIONAL MONUMENT IN 1961.
HUMANS SHELTERED IN THE CAVE
ROUGHLY 10,000 YEARS AGO BECAUSE
THE WATER INSIDE NEVER FROZE.

OVER 80% OF NEVADA'S LAND IS OWNED
BY THE FEDERAL GOVERNMENT.

FLOWING FOR 2,466 MILES THROUGH
SEVEN STATES, THE MISSOURI RIVER IS THE
LONGEST RIVER IN THE UNITED STATES.

ALONG HIGHWAY 95 IN
COTTONWOOD, IDAHO, YOU'LL
FIND THE DOG BARK INN –
A HOTEL BUILT IN THE SHAPE
OF A BEAGLE. LOCALS
AFFECTIONATELY CALL THE
PLACE "SWEET WILLY."

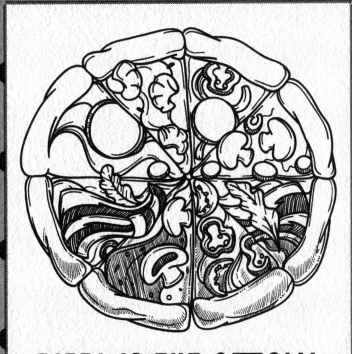

PIZZA IS THE OFFICIAL STATE FOOD OF CONNECTICUT.

MIRANDA RIGHTS FIRST CAME INTO
LAW IN ARIZONA IN 1966.

WYOMING IS THE MOST SPARSELY POPULATED
STATE WITH SOME 580,000 TOTAL RESIDENTS.

TEXAS HOLDS CLAIM TO 3,232 INTERSTATE
MILES-THE MOST IN THE NATION.

WHEN ROAD-TRIPPING THROUGH NORTH CAROLINA LOOK FOR THE UBIQUITOUS AND DELICIOUS CHEERWINE–A NON-ALCOHOLIC, CHERRY-FLAVORED FAVORITE.

THE GEOGRAPHIC CENTER OF THE U.S. IS JUST NORTH OF BELLE FOURCHE, SOUTH DAKOTA.

THE HIGHEST INTERSTATE NUMBER IS I-990 NORTH OF BUFFALO; THE LOWEST IS I-4 ACROSS FLORIDA.

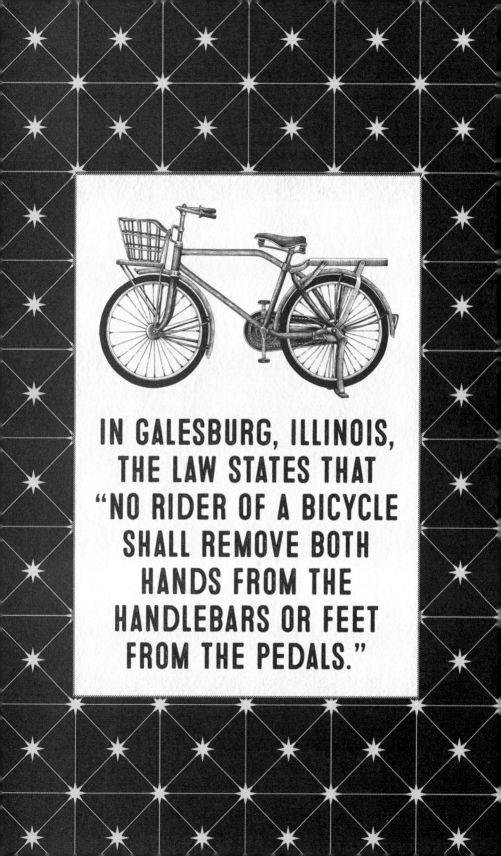

IN GALESBURG, ILLINOIS,
THE LAW STATES THAT
"NO RIDER OF A BICYCLE
SHALL REMOVE BOTH
HANDS FROM THE
HANDLEBARS OR FEET
FROM THE PEDALS."

IN REHOBOTH, DELAWARE
IT IS ILLEGAL TO
WHISPER IN CHURCH.

"BESSIE" THE LAKE ERIE MONSTER HAS BEEN SIGHTED OFF OHIO'S SHORELINE NUMEROUS TIMES OVER THE PAST 100 YEARS.

THE I-70 SECTION OF THE EISENHOWER TUNNEL IN THE COLORADO ROCKIES REACHES A PEAK HEIGHT OF 11,158 FEET— THE HIGHEST OF ALL INTERSTATES.

VERMONT'S OLDEST MARBLE QUARRY OPENED IN THE 1600S AND REMAINS IN OPERATION TODAY.

NORTH DAKOTA IS ONE OF THE
LEAST-VISITED STATES IN THE NATION.

MONTANA'S YELLOWSTONE RIVER IS
THE LONGEST UNDAMMED RIVER IN
THE U.S., RUNNING 700 MILES.

MILLS END PARK IN PORTLAND, OREGON,
MEASURES TWO FEET ACROSS, MAKING
IT THE SMALLEST PARK IN THE WORLD.

NORTH DAKOTA HAS
THE LEAST AMOUNT
OF FORESTED LAND
IN THE U.S.

THE FIG NEWTON
WAS FIRST BAKED
IN 1891 IN NEWTON,
MASSACHUSETTS.

JUSTIFICATION FOR BUILDING THE INTERSTATE
HIGHWAY SYSTEM IN THE 1950S AND 1960S
INCLUDED RAPID EVACUATION OF THE
CITIZENRY IN MAJOR CITIES IN
CASE OF A NUCLEAR ATTACK.

THE NEW RIVER GORGE BRIDGE IN WEST
VIRGINIA SPANS 1,700 FEET AND IS THE
LONGEST STEEL ARCH BRIDGE IN THE WORLD.

IF ALL THE DEER HUNTERS IN
WISCONSIN WERE GROUPED TOGETHER,
THEY WOULD COMPRISE THE SIXTH
LARGEST ARMY IN THE WORLD.

ASHLAND, NEBRASKA, HOSTS A
"TESTICLE FESTIVAL" EACH JUNE
AND SERVES MORE TESTICLES THAN
ANYWHERE ELSE IN THE WORLD.

SOUTH DAKOTA IS HOME TO BADLANDS
NATIONAL PARK. THE 244,000-ACRE MARVEL
FEATURES PINNACLES AND BUTTES RISING
FROM MIXED-GRASS PRAIRIE.

VERMONT HAS OVER 100 COVERED BRIDGES.

IN INDIANA IT'S UNLAWFUL TO THROW STONES AT A BIRD UNLESS IT'S IN SELF-DEFENSE.

**MONTANA HAS MORE
CATTLE THAN
HUMAN BEINGS.**

NEW YORK IS THE ONLY STATE
BORDERING BOTH THE GREAT LAKES
AND THE ATLANTIC OCEAN.

OHIO HAS THE LARGEST POPULATION
OF AMISH IN THE NATION.

VERMONT'S LAKE CHAMPLAIN IS SAID TO HAVE
A MONSTER NAMED "CHAMP" LURKING BELOW
THE SURFACE. DESPITE 300 REPORTED
SIGHTINGS, NO PHOTOGRAPHS OF CHAMP EXIST.

THE SECRET TRAIN STATION (TRACK 61) BELOW NEW YORK CITY'S WALDORF ASTORIA HOTEL WAS BUILT IN THE 1930S AS A SECRET ENTRANCE FOR PRESIDENT FRANKLIN D. ROOSEVELT.

THE BEAUTIFUL ROCKVILLE BRIDGE IN DAUPHIN COUNTY, PENNSYLVANIA, IS THE LONGEST STONE ARCH BRIDGE IN THE WORLD.

LAKE TAHOE, WHICH SHARES ITS SHORELINE WITH NEVADA AND CALIFORNIA, IS THE WORLD'S LARGEST ALPINE LAKE WITH 191 SQUARE MILES.

WASHINGTON
IS THE ONLY STATE
NAMED AFTER
A PRESIDENT.

REMOTE MORGAN ISLAND NEAR BEAUFORT, SOUTH CAROLINA, IS THE HOME OF A COLONY OF ROUGHLY 3,000 RHESUS MONKEYS.

TWINKIES WERE INVENTED IN
RIVER FOREST, ILLINOIS, IN 1930.

FIFTY PERCENT OF THE NATION'S
POPULATION LIVES WITHIN 500 MILES
OF COLUMBUS, OHIO.

NEW HAMPSHIRE PROHIBITS YOU
FROM TAKING SEAWEED OFF A BEACH.

THE STATUE OF LIBERTY IS COVERED
IN A LAYER OF COPPER A FRACTION OF
AN INCH THICK. OXIDATION OVER THE
YEARS HAS CHANGED HER BROWN COLOR
TO THE DISTINCTIVE GREEN SEEN TODAY.

WHITEWATER FALLS, SPANNING NORTH
AND SOUTH CAROLINA, IS THE TALLEST
WATERFALL IN THE EASTERN U.S.

THE ECLECTIC WOODMAN MUSEUM
IN DOVER, NEW HAMPSHIRE, DISPLAYS
EVERYTHING FROM ABE LINCOLN'S
SADDLE TO A FOUR-LEGGED CHICKEN.

NEVADA HAS
THE MOST ELVIS
IMPERSONATORS
IN THE U.S.

GRAND CANYON NATIONAL
PARK COULD FIT ALL
OF RHODE ISLAND IN IT
WITH 700,000 SQUARE
MILES TO SPARE.

LITTLE ROCK, ARKANSAS, IS HOME TO THE FAMED QUAPAW QUARTER RESTORATION PROJECT, FEATURING THE CITY'S OLDEST STRUCTURES INCLUDING ANTEBELLUM AND VICTORIAN HOMES, CHURCHES, THE OLD ARSENAL, AND MACARTHUR PARK.

TWENTY-FOUR MILES LONG, THE LAKE PONTCHARTRAIN CAUSEWAY IN LOUISIANA IS THE LONGEST BRIDGE OVER WATER IN THE WORLD.

THE PENTAGON IN ARLINGTON, VIRGINIA, IS THE LARGEST OFFICE BUILDING IN THE WORLD.

LOCATED IN ATLANTA, THE GEORGIA AQUARIUM IS THE LARGEST AQUARIUM IN THE ENTIRE U.S.

NEAR ASHEVILLE, NORTH CAROLINA, SPRAWLS THE MUST-VISIT, 8,000-ACRE, 250-ROOM BILTMORE ESTATE. OPEN TO EVERYONE TODAY, IT WAS ONCE THE PRIVATE ESTATE OF GEORGE VANDERBILT.

IDAHO'S NAME ORIGINATES FROM A NATIVE AMERICAN WORD MEANING, "THE LAND OF MANY WATERS."

THE TERM
"CHEESEBURGER"
WAS TRADEMARKED
IN DENVER, COLORADO.

NEAR KITTY HAWK,
NORTH CAROLINA, IS
KILL DEVIL HILLS WHERE
YOU CAN VISIT FIRST
FLIGHT AIRPORT AND
THE WRIGHT BROTHERS
NATIONAL MEMORIAL.

YOU CAN BOOK THE OPPORTUNITY TO
SWIM AND SNORKEL WITH MANATEES
AT FLORIDA'S HOMOSASSA WILDLIFE PARK.

IN COLORADO IT'S ILLEGAL TO OWN A
HOUSE WHERE UNMARRIED PERSONS
ARE ALLOWED TO HAVE SEX.

MAMOU, LOUISIANA, CALLS ITSELF
"THE CAJUN MUSIC CAPITAL OF THE WORLD."

ON HILTON ISLAND IN SOUTH CAROLINA YOU'LL FIND AN ANCIENT CIRCLE OF SEA SHELLS. THE SEA PINES SHELL RING IS THOUGHT TO HAVE BEEN CREATED BY INDIANS 4,000 YEARS AGO.

DENVER'S COLFAX AVENUE IS THE LONGEST CONTIGUOUS STREET IN THE U.S.

THE HAWAIIAN ALPHABET HAS ONLY 12 LETTERS.

CHURCH POINT, LOUISIANA, IS "THE BUGGY CAPITAL OF THE WORLD" AND HOSTS AN ANNUAL FESTIVAL THE FIRST WEEKEND OF JUNE.

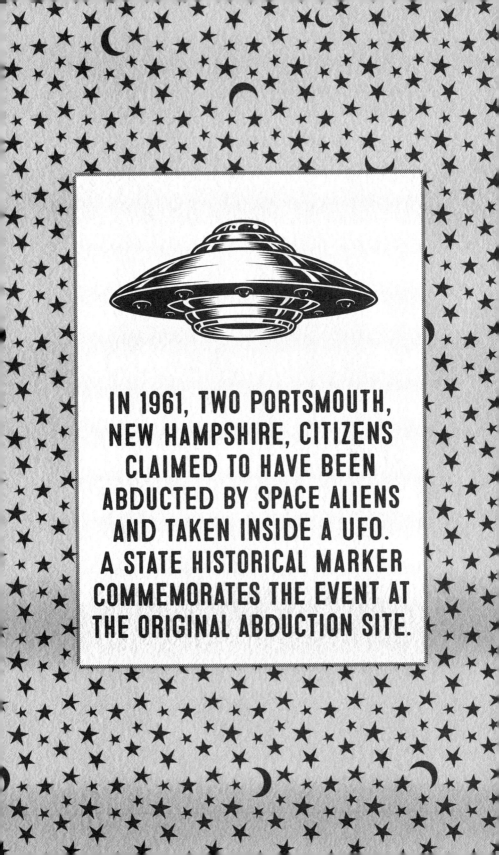

IN 1961, TWO PORTSMOUTH,
NEW HAMPSHIRE, CITIZENS
CLAIMED TO HAVE BEEN
ABDUCTED BY SPACE ALIENS
AND TAKEN INSIDE A UFO.
A STATE HISTORICAL MARKER
COMMEMORATES THE EVENT AT
THE ORIGINAL ABDUCTION SITE.

ROAD-TRIPPERS NEAR BISHOPVILLE, SOUTH CAROLINA, SHOULD BE ON THE LOOKOUT FOR THE "LIZARD MAN," A SCALY, SEVEN-FOOT-TALL CREATURE FIRST REPORTED IN 1988 TO HAVE ATTACKED A DISABLED VEHICLE, LEAVING DEEP SCRATCHES, NEAR SCAPE ORE SWAMP. OVER THE YEARS OTHERS HAVE COME FORWARD WITH SIMILAR STORIES.

THE NORTHERN LIGHTS ARE SEEN IN ALASKA ABOUT 250 DAYS EACH YEAR.

KENTUCKY'S MAMMOTH CAVE IN THE NATIONAL PARK OF THE SAME NAME IS ONE OF THE SEVEN NATURAL WONDERS OF THE WORLD.

IF THE FIRST DIGIT OF A THREE-DIGIT INTERSTATE NUMBER IS ODD, IT IS A SPUR INTO A CITY; IF EVEN, IT GOES THROUGH OR AROUND THE CITY.

DELLVIEW, NORTH CAROLINA, HAD JUST 13 RESIDENTS FOLLOWING THE LAST CENSUS.

DOOR COUNTY, WISCONSIN, HAS MORE SHORELINE (250 MILES) THAN ANY SINGLE COUNTY IN THE NATION.

THE EMPIRE STATE
BUILDING HAS ITS
OWN ZIP CODE.

IT IS ILLEGAL IN UTAH
TO FISH WHILE
ON HORSEBACK.

THE ARKANSAS STATE NAME IS DERIVED FROM THE FRENCH INTERPRETATION OF THE NATIVE AMERICAN WORD, "ACANSA", MEANING "DOWNSTREAM PLACE."

NEW ORLEANS, LOUISIANA, IS HOME TO THE MUST-VISIT WWII MUSEUM.

INTERSTATE HIGHWAY 95 RUNS THROUGH 16 STATES FROM MAINE TO FLORIDA-THE MOST STATES OF ANY INTERSTATE HIGHWAY.

THE GREENBRIER, LOCATED IN WEST VIRGINIA'S ALLEGHENY MOUNTAINS, IS ONE OF THE NATION'S MOST PRESTIGIOUS RESORTS AND FEATURES MORE THAN 700 GUEST ROOMS, 30 SOUVENIR SHOPS AND 20 RESTAURANTS.

VIRGINIA HAS 123 NATIONAL LANDMARKS.

BUC-EE'S IN NEW BRAUNFELS, TEXAS, IS THE WORLD'S LARGEST CONVENIENCE STORE WITH OVER 66,000 SQUARE FEET.

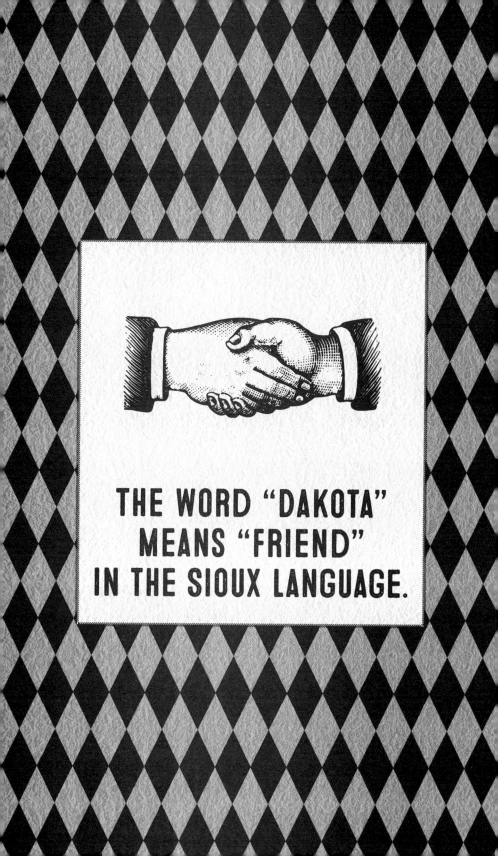

THE WORD "DAKOTA"
MEANS "FRIEND"
IN THE SIOUX LANGUAGE.

ARIZONA HAS 13 SPECIES
OF RATTLESNAKES.

IN 1903, HORATIO NELSON JACKSON MADE THE FIRST CROSS-COUNTRY ROAD TRIP BY AUTOMOBILE. THE JOURNEY FROM CALIFORNIA TO NEW YORK TOOK 63 DAYS.

AS THE CROW FLIES, MAINE IS THE CLOSEST STATE TO AFRICA.

THERE ARE MORE THAN 1,200 REST AREAS ON THE U.S. INTERSTATE HIGHWAY SYSTEM.

ONE WORLD TRADE CENTER IN NEW YORK CITY, IS THE TALLEST BUILDING IN THE U.S.

THE WANAMAKER ORGAN, LOCATED INSIDE MACY'S IN CENTER CITY, PHILADELPHIA, IS THE LARGEST OPERATIONAL PIPE ORGAN IN THE WORLD. FREE CONCERTS ARE GIVEN SIX DAYS A WEEK.

CARTOONIST JIM DAVIS HAILS FROM FAIRMONT, INDIANA, WHERE THE GARFIELD TRAIL HONORS HIS BELOVED FELINE CHARACTER WITH MORE THAN A DOZEN STATUES.

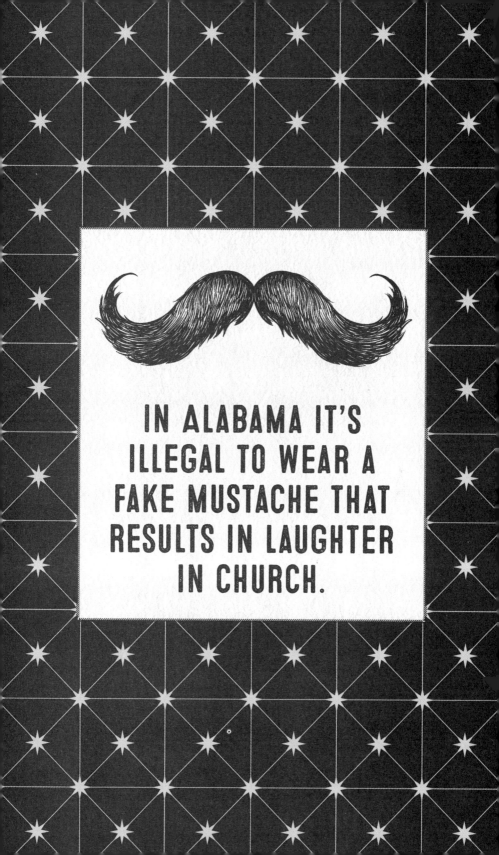

IN ALABAMA IT'S
ILLEGAL TO WEAR A
FAKE MUSTACHE THAT
RESULTS IN LAUGHTER
IN CHURCH.

REPTILES BY LAW MUST
BE KEPT AT LEAST 200
YARDS AWAY FROM THE
MARDI GRAS PARADE
ROUTE IN NEW ORLEANS.

IN TOMBSTONE, ARIZONA, IT IS ILLEGAL FOR MEN AND WOMEN OVER THE AGE OF 18 TO HAVE A MISSING TOOTH VISIBLE WHEN SMILING.

OHIO'S BUSH CREEK VALLEY FEATURES THE HALF-MILE-LONG GREAT SERPENT MOUND, THE LARGEST SERPENT EFFIGY IN THE WORLD.

IN 1901, NEW YORK BECAME THE FIRST STATE REQUIRING LICENSE PLATES FOR AUTOMOBILES.

IOWA IS USUALLY ASSOCIATED WITH CORN, BUT ITS FERTILE SOIL ALSO PRODUCES LOVELY GRAPES. 358,000 TOURISTS ANNUALLY VISIT THE STATE'S 100 WINERIES AND TASTING ROOMS.

YOU CAN FIND "CARHENGE," AN AUTOMOTIVE REPLICA OF THE ENGLISH STONEHENGE, JUST NORTH OF ALLIANCE, NEBRASKA.

MONTANA'S ROE RIVER RUNS 201 FEET, MAKING IT THE SHORTEST RIVER IN THE WORLD.

SINCE 1933, ORANGE CITY, IOWA, HAS HELD AN ANNUAL TULIP FESTIVAL FEATURING PARADES, FLORAL SHOWS, ART, MUSIC AND DUTCH FOODS THAT PAY TRIBUTE TO THE EARLY DUTCH SETTLERS.

IN NORFOLK, VIRGINIA,
IT'S ILLEGAL TO SPIT
ON A SEAGULL.

UTAH BARS AND RESTAURANTS HAVE
PARTITIONS SEPARATING BARTENDERS
FROM THEIR CUSTOMERS. DUBBED
"ZION CURTAINS" THEY'RE INTENDED
TO PREVENT EXCESSIVE DRINKING.

THE WORLD'S LARGEST HOT-AIR BALLOON
FESTIVAL IS HELD EVERY OCTOBER
IN ALBUQUERQUE, NEW MEXICO.

THE WORLD GOLF HALL OF FAME IS
IN ST. JOHNS COUNTY, FLORIDA.

GEORGIA'S FAMED BLUE RIDGE MOUNTAINS
HIGHEST PEAK TOWERS 4,785 FEET.

PORTLAND, OREGON, HAS MORE BREWERIES
THAN ANY CITY ON EARTH. IT ALSO HAS
THE MOST STRIP CLUBS PER CAPITA.

CALIFORNIA'S HIGHEST POINT (MT. WHITNEY)
AND LOWEST POINT (DEATH VALLEY)
ARE ONLY 85 MILES APART.

DENNY'S RESTAURANT IN LAS VEGAS ALSO OFFERS WEDDING SERVICES.

DOG MUSHING IS
ALASKA'S STATE SPORT.

IN WATERLOO, NEBRASKA, BARBERS
ARE FORBIDDEN FROM EATING ONIONS
FROM 7:00 A.M. TO 7:00 P.M.

AT 7,708 FEET, WASHINGTON STATE'S
EVERGREEN POINT FLOATING BRIDGE
IS THE LONGEST SUCH STRUCTURE IN
THE WORLD. IT CONNECTS SEATTLE TO
BELLEVUE ACROSS LAKE WASHINGTON.

THE KENNEDY SPACE CENTER IN CAPE
CANAVERAL IS AN ACTIVE SPACE
CENTER AND WELCOMES VISITORS.

BLUE JEANS WERE FIRST MADE IN RENO, NEVADA, BY TAILOR JACOB DAVIS IN 1870. SEVERAL YEARS LATER HE PARTNERED WITH DENIM SUPPLIER LEVI STRAUSS.

SPRINGFIELD, OREGON, IS THE REAL LIFE INSPIRATION FOR THE TV SIMPSON'S HOMETOWN OF THE SAME NAME.

THE "LONELIEST ROAD IN AMERICA" RUNS 408 MILES ON NEVADA'S ROUTE 50.

IT'S ILLEGAL IN FLORIDA
FOR FOOD TRUCK
VENDORS TO DRESS
PROVOCATIVELY.

THE NEBRASKA "SHOE FENCE" IS ADORNED WITH UPSIDE DOWN BOOTS AND SHOES AND RUNS ON HIGHWAY 26 FOR MILES BETWEEN NORTHPORT AND OGALLALA.

THE FLORA-BAMA LOUNGE, LOCATED ON THE ORANGE BEACH, ALABAMA, AND PERDIDO KEY, FLORIDA, LINE, HOLDS AN ANNUAL "MULLET TOSS"–AN ANNUAL EVENT SINCE 1985.

THE DIBBLE HOUSE IN ELDON, IOWA, WAS THE BACKDROP FOR THE ICONIC PAINTING, AMERICAN GOTHIC, BY GRANT WOOD IN 1930.

THOUGH IT OPENED BACK IN 1992, MINNEAPOLIS, MINNESOTA'S MALL OF AMERICA REMAINS THE LARGEST SUCH SHOPPING MECCA IN THE COUNTRY.

DON'T MISS NORTH DAKOTA'S ENCHANTED
HIGHWAY OFFERING HUGE METAL SCULPTURES
ALONG A 32-MILE STRETCH FROM EXIT 72 ON
I-94 IN GLADSTONE TO THE TOWN OF REGENT.

BULLET HOLES ARE STILL SEEN IN THE
ST. JAMES HOTEL IN CIMARRON,
NEW MEXICO, WHERE 26 MURDERS
OCCURRED BACK IN THE WILD WEST DAYS.

COLORADO IS THE ONLY STATE TO TURN DOWN
THE OPPORTUNITY TO HOST THE OLYMPICS.

PARK COUNTY, INDIANA,
CONTAINS 31 HISTORIC
COVERED BRIDGES.

THE TOWN OF SANTA CLAUS, INDIANA, ESTABLISHED IN 1856, HAS BECOME KNOWN AS AMERICA'S CHRISTMAS HOMETOWN.

VISIT THE "FOUR CORNERS MONUMENT" AND STAND WHERE THE STATES OF NEW MEXICO, COLORADO, UTAH, AND ARIZONA MEET. IN NEW MEXICO IT IS FOUND ON THE NAVAJO INDIAN RESERVATION IN SAN JUAN COUNTY.

IN WEST VIRGINIA IT'S LEGAL TO TAKE HOME ROADKILL.

THE LOST RIVER CAVE BENEATH BOWLING GREEN, KENTUCKY, OFFERS A SEVEN-MILE CAVE SYSTEM AND FEATURES BOAT AND KAYAK TOURS.

IN IDAHO, HELLS CANYON AT 7,900 FEET DEEP
IS DEEPER THAN THE GRAND CANYON.

PRUDHOE BAY IS THE NORTHERNMOST POINT
TO WHICH YOU CAN DRIVE IN ALASKA.

TEXAS PETE HOT SAUCE IS NOT
FROM TEXAS BUT NORTH CAROLINA.

AUSTIN, TEXAS, IS THE "MUSIC CAPITAL OF THE WORLD."

IN RICHMOND, VIRGINIA,
IT'S ILLEGAL TO FLIP
A COIN OVER WHO
BUYS THE COFFEE.

KANSAS NATIVE REV. SYLVESTER GRAHAM INVENTED THE GRAHAM CRACKER IN 1829.

DR PEPPER WAS INVENTED IN WACO, TEXAS, IN 1885. THE ORIGINAL SECRET RECIPE IS CUT IN TWO HALVES AND STORED IN SAFE DEPOSIT BOXES IN TWO SEPARATE DALLAS BANKS.

THE LONGEST INTERSTATE HIGHWAY (I-90) STRETCHES 3,085 CONTIGUOUS MILES FROM SEATTLE TO BOSTON.

OVER FIVE MILES LONG, THE ATLANTIC CITY
BOARDWALK IS BOTH THE OLDEST
AND LONGEST IN THE U.S.

SONIC DRIVE-IN WAS FOUNDED
IN SHAWNEE, OKLAHOMA.

THE WHITE HORSE TAVERN IN NEWPORT,
RHODE ISLAND, HAS BEEN SERVING CUSTOMERS
SINCE ORIGINALLY OPENING IN 1673.

DELAWARE HAS
200 TIMES
MORE CHICKENS
THAN PEOPLE.

THE FIRST DUNKIN DONUTS SHOP OPENED IN QUINCY, MASSACHUSETTS, IN 1948.

NEVADA'S STATE ROUTE 375 IS CALLED THE "EXTRATERRESTRIAL HIGHWAY" AND RUNS 98 MILES ACROSS THE DESERT WHERE MANY UFO SIGHTINGS HAVE BEEN REPORTED.

MYSTICAL HORIZONS, KNOWN AS THE "NORTH DAKOTA STONEHENGE," IS JUST OFF HIGHWAY 43 NEAR BOTTINEAU, NORTH DAKOTA.

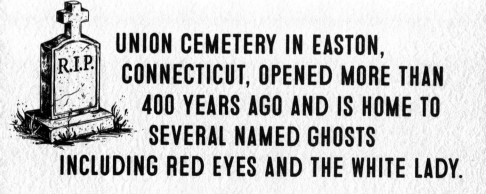

UNION CEMETERY IN EASTON, CONNECTICUT, OPENED MORE THAN 400 YEARS AGO AND IS HOME TO SEVERAL NAMED GHOSTS INCLUDING RED EYES AND THE WHITE LADY.

NEARLY 80% OF ILLINOIS IS FARMLAND.

66% OF MISSOURI'S LAND MASS IS OCCUPIED BY NEARLY 10,000 FARMS.

PERRY COUNTY, PENNSYLVANIA, IS HOME TO ONE OF THE OLDEST ORGANISMS IN THE WORLD. THE LOSH RUN BOX HUCKLEBERRY IS ROUGHLY 13,000 YEARS OLD.

IN EXCELSIOR, MISSOURI,
IT'S ILLEGAL TO
WORRY SQUIRRELS.

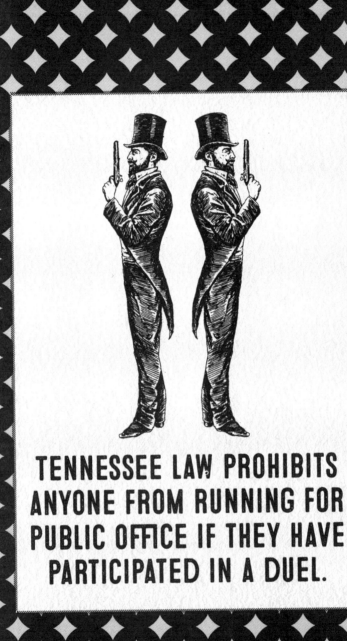

TENNESSEE LAW PROHIBITS ANYONE FROM RUNNING FOR PUBLIC OFFICE IF THEY HAVE PARTICIPATED IN A DUEL.

THE GOLDEN GATE BRIDGE IS NOT GOLDEN, BUT INTERNATIONAL ORANGE.

PEPSI-COLA WAS INVENTED IN 1893 BY A NEW BERN, NORTH CAROLINA, DRUGGIST.

MIDDLESBORO, KENTUCKY, IS THE ONLY TOWN BUILT INSIDE A METEOR CRATER.

SEATTLE'S SPACE NEEDLE WAS BUILT
FOR THE 1962 WORLD'S FAIR.

STEALING AN ALLIGATOR IN LOUISIANA
CAN GET YOU 10 YEARS IN PRISON.

FOUNDED IN 1634, BOSTON COMMON IS
THE OLDEST PUBLIC PARK IN THE COUNTRY.

THE GRAND OLE OPRY FEATURES
THE LONGEST-RUNNING RADIO
SHOW IN THE WORLD AND
IS A "MUST VISIT" FOR
MUSIC-LOVING ROAD-TRIPPERS.

IN 1879 CLEVELAND, OHIO,
BECAME THE FIRST CITY TO
BE LIT BY ELECTRICITY.

LIFE SAVERS CANDY WAS INVENTED
IN GARRETSVILLE, OHIO, IN 1912.

JUST OUTSIDE OF RUGBY, NORTH DAKOTA,
YOU'LL FIND THE PRAIRIE VILLAGE MUSEUM
FEATURING THE "WORLD'S TALLEST SALESMAN"
DISPLAY, STUFFED BOXING ALLIGATORS, AND
THE WORLD'S SECOND-LARGEST BELT BUCKLE.
OPEN MAY THROUGH OCTOBER.

IOWA'S MAQUOKETA CAVES STATE PARK
INCLUDES 13 CAVES OPEN TO THE PUBLIC.

MINNESOTA IS CALLED THE
"LAND OF 10,000 LAKES," BUT THE
REAL NUMBER IS CLOSER TO 12,000.

THE WORLD'S RECORD ENCHILADA
(10 FEET LONG) WAS CRAFTED IN
LAS CRUCES, NEW MEXICO.

NEVADA HAS THE LARGEST WILD HORSE
POPULATION IN THE NATION.

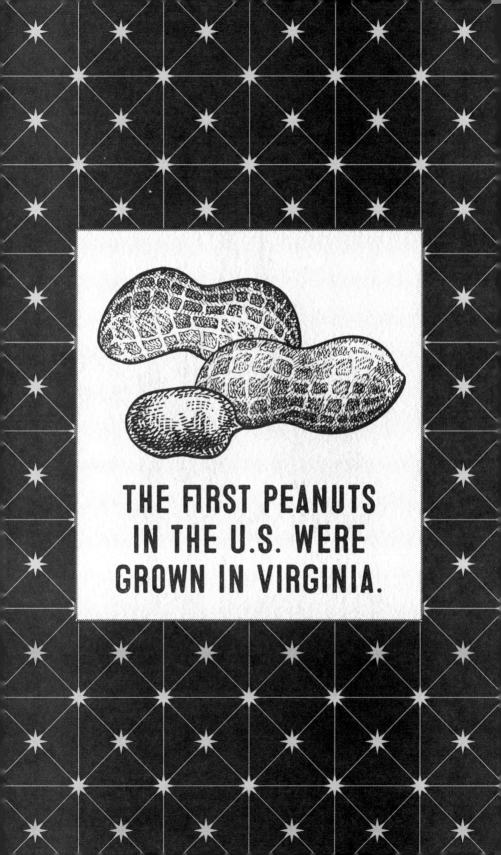

THE FIRST PEANUTS
IN THE U.S. WERE
GROWN IN VIRGINIA.

58 MILLION PEOPLE VISIT FLORIDA'S WALT DISNEY RESORT EACH YEAR.